LIVING LEGENDS OF SPORTS

MIKE TROUT

BASEBALL MVP

MARTY GITLIN

Britannica
Educational Publishing
IN ASSOCIATION WITH
ROSEN
EDUCATIONAL SERVICES

Published in 2019 by Britannica Educational Publishing (a trademark of Encyclopædia Britannica, Inc.) in association with The Rosen Publishing Group, Inc.
29 East 21st Street, New York, NY 10010

Distributed exclusively by Rosen Publishing.
To see additional Britannica Educational Publishing titles, go to rosenpublishing.com.

First Edition

Britannica Educational Publishing
J. E. Luebering: Executive Director, Core Editorial
Andrea R. Field: Managing Editor, Compton's by Britannica

Rosen Publishing
Kathy Kuhtz Campbell: Senior Editor
Nelson Sá: Art Director
Nicole Russo-Duca: Series Designer and Book Layout
Cindy Reiman: Photography Manager
Sherri Jackson: Photo Researcher

Library of Congress Cataloging-in-Publication Data

Names: Gitlin, Marty, author.
Title: Mike Trout: baseball MVP / Marty Gitlin.
Description: New York: Britannica Educational Publishing, in Association with Rosen Educational Services, 2019. | Series: Living Legends of Sports | Includes bibliographical references and index. | Audience: Grades 5–8.
Identifiers: LCCN 2017050762| ISBN 9781538302200 (library bound) | ISBN 9781538302217 (paperback)
Subjects: LCSH: Trout, Mike, 1991—Juvenile literature. | Baseball players—United States—Biography—Juvenile literature.
Classification: LCC GV865.T73 G57 2019 | DDC 796.357092 [B] —dc23
LC record available at https://lccn.loc.gov/2017050762

Manufactured in the United States of America

Photo credits: Cover, p. 1 Bob Levey/Getty Images; cover and interior pages background © iStockphoto/stevezmina1; p. 5 Mark Cunningham/Getty Images; p. 6 Matt Brown/Getty Images; p. 7 ZUMA Press, Inc./Alamy Stock Photo; pp. 8-9, 16, 17, 25, 26-27, 30 © AP Images; pp. 10-11 WENN Ltd/Alamy Stock Photo; pp. 12-13, 18-19 Jeff Gross/Getty Images; pp. 20-21 Victor Decolongon /Getty Images; p. 22 Otto Greule Jr/Getty Images; p. 24 Uschi Gerschner/Newscom; p. 28 Patrick Smith/Getty Images; p. 32 Icon Sportswire/Getty Images; p. 33 Rob Tringali/SportsChrome/Getty Images; p. 34 Angels Baseball LP/Getty Images; p. 36 Matt Brown /Getty Images; p. 37 Harry How/Getty Images.

CONTENTS

OUT
0 9
3
2
1
INNING 1 2 3 4 5 6 7 8 9 10 R H E
VISITOR 2 0 4 0 0 7 0 1 0 0 1 4 9 1
HOME 0 5 0 0 0 0 0 0 2 1 0 8 6 3

INTRODUCTION

Mike Trout can do everything on a baseball field. The term "five-tool player" describes his talent perfectly. He hits for average and power, runs like the wind, covers center field, and throws the ball with strength and accuracy.

Most people agree that he is the most talented player in the game. He has been consistently great since his rookie season of 2012. He plays in the media spotlight of Los Angeles, California. He boasts an engaging personality. He is likable.

So why is Mike Trout not the face of baseball? Why do fans not see him in dozens of commercials?

The answer is simple. He does not want the attention. Trout is too modest to grab it. He was raised by his parents to be humble. He prefers spending time with friends in his hometown of Millville, New Jersey, to flying around the country making more money. Why else would he have continued to live with his parents after signing a $144-million contract?

Trout is not driven by fame and fortune, but they come with the territory. They come with his greatness as a baseball player. Anyone who finishes near the top of the Most Valuable Player (MVP) vote every year and wins the award twice is destined for recognition. Trout does not seek the spotlight. He just earns it.

Mike Trout's speed allows him to slide safely ahead of the tag by Detroit Tigers catcher Brayan Pena in a 2013 victory of the Los Angeles Angels of Anaheim over the Tigers.

CHAPTER ONE

Home Sweet Home

Rookie pitcher Mike Morin would never forget the moment. Spring training was nearing an end. Morin was hoping to land a spot with the Los Angeles Angels. It was a sizzling hot afternoon in Arizona.

Superstar teammate Mike Trout approached him in the locker room, according to baseball columnist Peter Gammons. "Want to play golf this afternoon?" he asked. Morin replied that it would take time to retrieve his

Mike Trout is a great ambassador for the sport of baseball. He spends a lot of time interacting with fans and signing autographs.

golf clubs, eat, and shower. Trout had a solution. He would take Morin's food order and pick it up. He would then bring it to the golf course.

Trout had broken baseball tradition. The best players in the world do not cater to rookies. They do not carry their bags in hotels. They do not get their lunches. But Trout is different. He is humble. He does not feel superior to anyone, and Morin appreciated it.

Mike is flanked by his parents, Jeff and Debbie Trout, at an event at the Empire State Building in New York City.

"That's all anyone needs to know about Mike Trout," he said, according to Gammons. "He's the best player in the game ... [and] I'm trying to make the team. And he's taking my order and picking up my food so we can play together. He has no air of being a star. He's just the most normal person you could ever meet."

That praise would surprise nobody in Millville, New Jersey. That is where Michael Nelson Trout was raised after his birth on August 7, 1991, in nearby Vineland. Those in the small community speak glowingly about Trout. They praise him for remaining modest despite his wealth and fame.

They thank his parents, Jeff and Debbie Trout. The two former schoolteachers brought their son up to be humble. Jeff taught American and world

QUICK FACT

Mike Trout's father was a fine hitter in the minor leagues. Jeff owned a career batting average of .303. He played his last three seasons at the Double-A level before retiring.

history at Millville High School while coaching the baseball and football teams. Debbie served as a teaching aide for young children.

Dad Was a Ballplayer

Mike has baseball in his blood. His father played four minor league seasons in the Minnesota Twins system. He retired after realizing he was not going to reach the big leagues. He became a family man, one who yearned to raise Mike as best as he and his wife could.

The result was a tight family with high moral standards. Former Angels scouting director Eddie Bane learned all about the

Mike Trout poses with a former Millville High School classmate before a game in Philadelphia, Pennsylvania, in 2014.

ANGELS

Trouts when he scouted Mike. He came away impressed.

"It's like a Disney movie," Bane told Bob Nightengale of *USA TODAY* Sports. "The family is so close-knit. Everyone talks about what a great, young, polite kid Mike is. Well, once you know the family, you see where he gets it from."

How tight are the Trouts? Mike could afford to spend his off-seasons anywhere in the world after signing a six-year contract worth $144 million with the Angels in 2014. But he returned home every year to live with his parents.

Mike seemed destined for greatness as a standout at Millville High School. He began his career as a pitcher and shortstop. His brilliance was evident immediately. Trout batted .338 with 14 stolen bases as a mere freshman. During his sophomore season he batted .457 and racked up 79 strikeouts in 54 innings pitched. He threw four shutouts, including a no-hitter, as a junior while raising his batting average to .530. He led his team in home runs and runs batted in (RBI).

Trout and his parents take part in a ceremony with Millville High School's varsity baseball team at the Empire State Building in New York City in 2013. The ceremony celebrated the dedication of Mike Trout Field at Millville High School.

Trout bolts out of the batter's box during the 2010 All-Star Futures Game at Angels Stadium in Anaheim, California.

Trout had grown by that time. He was a small contact hitter when he began his high school career. He was not a huge player by his senior season. But his standout power excited scouts. His combination of speed and strength was unique for a 17-year-old.

QUICK FACT

Trout also played football and basketball in high school. He totaled 14 points and 18 rebounds in one basketball game during his senior year.

Best of the Best

By that time, Trout was ranked as the top prospect in New Jersey. His blazing speed had earned him the nickname "the Millville Meteor." More scouts than fans attended his games his senior year. Among them was Angels scout Greg Morhardt. He was quite familiar with the Trout family. He played on the same minor league team as Jeff. And he was quite impressed with Jeff's son.

"He was much faster than everyone in the country," Morhardt told Fox Sports reporter Ken Rosenthal. "He was much stronger than everyone in the country. He had the timing, the instincts. ... He was stronger than any 17-year-old I'd ever seen."

Morhardt, according to Rosenthal, told Ric Wilson, who was another Angels scout: "We've got to get Trout."

It reached the point where Morhardt wished Trout would make outs so he would not impress other

QUICK FACT

The Cherry Hill East High School team was so scared of Trout that it once walked him intentionally with the bases loaded. Trout was intentionally walked three times in the game. The strategy worked, as Cherry Hill East defeated Millville.

scouts. He wanted Trout to pop the ball up. But every time Trout did send the ball high in the sky, he showed off his speed running to first base. Morhardt could only hope he was the only one that realized how great a prospect he was watching.

There was another problem. Trout had committed to East Carolina University (ECU) when he realized he was good enough to play college baseball. He would have a decision to make after he was drafted by a Major League Baseball (MLB) team. But that decision would prove to be quite easy. Trout had outplayed the need to hone his skills at the college level.

That fact was not lost on ECU coach Billy Godwin. He got the message loud and clear by watching Trout play. He noted that many major league scouts were also in attendance. As reported by Jason Mazda of the *Press of Atlantic City*, he witnessed Trout circling the bases for an inside-the-park home run on a ball that landed *in front* of the center fielder.

Godwin knew then and there that Trout was too talented to reject the money he would be offered by a major league team. "That's the best high school player I've ever seen," Godwin told Millville baseball coach Roy Hallenbeck, according to Mazda. "He ain't coming to East Carolina."

He was right. Trout would soon be stealing bases and smashing line drives as the best minor league prospect in baseball. The only mystery remaining was which team would be smart enough to draft him.

CHAPTER TWO

Minor League Marvel

Mike Trout had one problem heading into the 2009 MLB Draft. He was from New Jersey. The top players are most often from warm-weather states such as Florida, Texas, and California. They compete year-round.

Some scouts could not believe that the tiny town of Millville could produce a star. They had done their homework. They knew about Trout. But they feared that any player from the Northeast was a great risk. So they passed on him.

> **QUICK FACT**
>
> Only two players drafted before Trout in 2009 have starred in the major leagues. They are Washington Nationals pitcher Stephen Strasburg and Arizona Diamondbacks outfielder A. J. Pollock.

One team after another selected players with lesser talent. Trout's father thought Seattle might take him with the second overall pick. Oakland also seemed interested. But those teams chose other players. And that made Angels scout Greg Morhardt very happy. He had issued a glowing report on Trout. He was hoping other teams would shy away.

"There were only two players I've ever scouted where I put in the report that they had a chance to be a Hall of Fame player," Morhardt

Major League Baseball commissioner Bud Selig announces a selection during the 2009 draft at the MLB Network studios. Trout and his parents attended the event in Secaucus, New Jersey.

told Bob Nightengale. "One was [New York Mets pitcher] Matt Harvey. The other was Mikey. He had the strongest and fastest combination I've ever seen. I was just praying that no one would draft him."

According to Rosenthal, Mike and his parents attended the draft at the MLB Network studios. Trout was the only player to show up. His parents dreaded the embarrassment of being on camera if Mike dropped to the second round. Finally, the Angels grabbed him at number 25 in the first round.

Trout would soon make every team that picked before the Angels very sorry. He took baseball by storm. He batted .360 in the rookie-level Arizona League in 2009 before being moved up the next year to Class A Cedar Rapids.

It was there he began to display the speed and power that would make him a young legend. Trout was batting an amazing .366 early that year when many called for another promotion. He spoke about biding

Trout happily holds up an Angels jersey beside Commissioner Selig after being chosen by the Los Angeles Angels in the first round of the 2009 draft.

his time and simply playing his best. Cedar Rapids Kernels manager Bill Mosiello hoped he would stick around for a while. After all, Trout was still young.

"What is the plus of him moving up?" Mosiello asked Jeff Johnson of the *Gazette*. "He's an 18-year-old. Why rush his progression? If he was 21 or 22, then maybe you would see, 'Hey, maybe he could play in the big leagues in a year.' But you're 18, there's nothing to be gained. I don't really see the need to get him out of here."

Onward and Upward

The Angels did see the need. They soon sent Trout to Advanced Class A Rancho Cucamonga. He finished the 2010 season with a .341 batting average, 56 stolen bases, and 106 runs scored. It came as little surprise when he won the J. G. Taylor Spink Award as the best player in the minor leagues.

Trout had yet to show the power he would display in the majors. That became evident in 2011 at Double-A Arkansas. Trout was batting .308 with a .415 on-base percentage by late May. He had scored 28 runs and stolen nine bases in just 39 games. The Angels desperately needed outfield help. Their fans screamed for them to send for Trout. Never mind that he was only 19 years old.

Most minor leaguers never reach the majors. Most top prospects drafted out of high school receive at least five years of minor league seasoning. Trout had played less than two years. Angels manager Mike Scioscia praised him while warning that rushing him could be harmful.

"I think that's a huge risk with a player with his upside,"

QUICK FACT

Trout was named Minor League Player of the Year by *Baseball America* in 2011.

Speedy Mike Trout slides safely into second base as Florida Marlins prospect Ozzie Martinez awaits the throw during the 2010 All-Star Futures Game.

NGA
ASIN

Scioscia told Mike DiGiovanna of the *Los Angeles Times*. "We see the growth in Mike. He's made an incredible amount of progress from last year to now ... There are a lot of things he'll benefit from in the minor leagues that will give him a better chance when he's ready for the big leagues ... Right now, he's not an option."

He was certainly an option two months later. Trout had raised his average to .330 with nine home runs and 28 stolen bases. The Angels had lost outfielder Peter Bourjos to a hamstring injury on July 7, 2011. Scioscia and general manager Tony Reagins weighed their choices. They decided to promote Trout to the big leagues.

A Slow Start

Trout understood that all eyes would be upon him once he arrived. But he also knew that playing his first major league game that night would bring him comfort. "There's always going to be pressure," he told the Associated Press. "Once you get on the field, it's just a game. Tonight is going to be a thrill, and I can't wait."

Trout went 0-for-3 at the plate in his debut game against the

Playing center field for the Angels, Trout tracks down a ball for a catch in the ninth inning of a July 2011 victory over American League West rival Seattle.

Mike Trout displays the batting stance and concentration that have helped make him one of the greatest hitters in baseball.

Seattle Mariners on July 8. (The Angels won 4–3.) He began to struggle for the first time in his baseball life. He managed just four hits in his first 30 at-bats with no home runs or stolen bases. The return to health of Bourjos signaled the end of his brief stay in Los Angeles. Trout was demoted back to Double-A Arkansas on August 1.

QUICK FACT

According to Ben Lindbergh of the Ringer, Angels scout Eddie Bane claimed that Trout was timed at a blazing 3.9 seconds running to first base in a minor league all-star game.

He did not stay long. He returned to the Angels in less than three weeks and showed signs of brilliance. He put together a six-game hitting streak. He blasted two home runs in a game against Seattle. But a 3-for-38 slide shrunk his average to .207 in late September.

Trout would have to wait until 2012 to prove his greatness. The 19-year-old had been a bit too eager. He showed little plate discipline. He swung at too many pitches outside the strike zone. But his teammates and opponents could see his potential. Among them was Angels pitcher Dan Haren. He cited the two-homer game against the Mariners as a reason to be hopeful.

"I remember thinking how unique his swing was and how the ball just jumped off his bat," Haren told Ben Lindbergh of the Ringer. "There was never a point even with his early struggles that any of us thought that he wasn't legit. I had never played with anyone with that combination of speed and power."

The baseball world would not have to wait much longer to see that speed and power destroy opponents. Trout was soon transformed from prospect to one of the best players in baseball. But his 2012 season did not begin with a bang.

CHAPTER THREE

Most Valuable Mike

Some players get sick of spring training. They think it is too long. In 2012, Mike Trout got sick *in* spring training. And it was not long enough.

A lingering virus caused Trout to lose 20 pounds. He also suffered from shoulder tendinitis that prevented him from throwing. He was limited to just six at-bats before the regular season. That punched his ticket back

Bumble, the mascot of the Triple-A Salt Lake Bees, cheers the crowd at a Bees home game in Salt Lake City, Utah. Trout played for the Bees on the way to baseball greatness.

Budding star Mike Trout hustles to first base during a 2012 Angels game against the Indians in Cleveland.

to the minors. He started the season playing Triple-A ball with the Salt Lake Bees in Salt Lake City.

Some fans grew concerned that Trout was too young to thrive in the big leagues. After all, he had struggled with the Angels in 2011. They remained skeptical even after Trout dominated minor league pitching to start 2012. He batted .403 and led the Pacific Coast League in triples and runs scored.

Trout was promoted again on April 28. He quickly washed away all doubts. Scioscia placed him in the leadoff spot to take advantage of his speed and ability to reach base. The manager vowed to play Trout every day. He was going to let the kid with the last name of a fish sink or swim.

Trout answers a reporter's question during a news conference in Millville after being named 2012 American League Rookie of the Year.

Boy, did Trout swim. He slugged at least two hits in nine of his first 17 games in May to raise his average to .355.

Trout remained hot the rest of the season. He finished it with 30 home runs. He led the American League with 129 runs scored and 49 stolen bases. He won the American League MLB Rookie of the Year award in a unanimous vote. He finished second to Detroit slugger Miguel Cabrera in the MVP balloting.

Trout was the talk of baseball. He landed on the cover of *Sports Illustrated* in late August. Teammates, coaches, and opponents raved about him.

Among them was Baltimore Orioles manager Buck Showalter. Showalter had been in professional baseball for 35 years. He knew talent, and he was in awe of Trout. He expressed his feelings after the young phenom had slammed four hits and reached over the wall to rob an Orioles player of a home run.

"There's nothing not to like about Trout," Showalter told Kevin Baxter of the *Los Angeles Times*. "He's a very physical baseball player. You see him and you go, 'Good God' … Trout's special … He's going to impact a game in all the phases."

He's safe! Trout slides under the tag of Nationals catcher Jóse Lobatón in the sixth inning of an April 2014 game in Washington, DC.

Remaining on a Roll

What amazed everyone was Trout's consistent brilliance. He rarely slumped. Opponents that hoped 2012 was a one-year wonder received a jolt of reality. He was even better in 2013. He became more patient at the plate as some pitchers refused to throw him strikes. The result was a league-leading 110 walks. His on-base percentage (OBP) soared to .432.

Trout did not allow pitchers fearful of throwing strikes to ruin his production. He bashed a career-high 39 doubles and led the American League with 109 runs scored. The All-Star again placed second to Cabrera in the MVP voting. He might have won it had the Angels not finished under .500.

By the end of that season Trout was already considered among the best players in history. His career wins above replacement (WAR) had risen to 19.1. The metric is used to measure overall production. It compares how many games a team wins with a particular player to what its win total would be if that player was replaced by an average player.

The *Hardball Times* writer Jason Linden used WAR to argue in late August 2013 that Trout might be the best ever at his age. He claimed that players with a career WAR of 60 are generally inducted into the Hall of Fame. Trout was nearly one-third of the way there in just two full seasons.

He had knocked on the MVP door in both years. He bashed it down in 2014. His statistics were no better than they were in 2013. His batting average fell to a career-low .287. But Trout led the league in runs scored and RBI while smashing 36 home runs. The difference was that his Angels won 98 games and the division title. Trout earned all 30 first-place MVP votes.

His greatness continued to be shown in the balloting for that award. He placed second in the voting in 2015 and won it in 2016. Trout earned the award in 2016 even though the Angels again finished the season well under .500. No player in baseball compiled better offensive numbers.

QUICK FACT

Trout has never been part of a playoff victory. His Angels were swept by Kansas City in his first 2014 American League Division Series. He managed just one hit in 12 at-bats. But it was a home run.

Dandy Defender

But Trout had earned a reputation as more than an amazing hitter. He became established as a five-tool player. That means he could hit for average and power, but he could also run, throw, and field. He robbed frustrated hitters of home runs by leaping to catch balls headed over the fence.

He turned so many homers into outs that his best effort has been debated. Some believe his finest was achieved in Baltimore on June 27, 2012. Orioles slugger J. J. Hardy launched a pitch high and deep into center field. Trout raced back. He had no time to stop and time his jump. He leaped off a full sprint and reached his arm over the fence. He caught the ball in the tip of his glove.

Mike Trout remarkably robs Orioles slugger J. J. Hardy of a home run in a June 2012 game in Baltimore.

Trout then displayed the joy he receives from playing the sport and helping his team. He pumped his fist and broke out in a wide smile. That play in his rookie year would be just one of his many incredible defensive efforts. Trout will be forever known for his booming bat and great speed on the bases. But he takes equal pride in his defense.

QUICK FACT

Trout lost about seven weeks to a left thumb injury in 2017. He was out of the lineup from the end of May to mid-July. The Angels managed a record of 19–20 without him.

That defense had through 2017 not earned Trout any Gold Glove awards. Trout made no errors in 2015, yet failed to win one. That upset Scioscia. He believed that the statistics used to help determine Gold Glove winners were flawed.

"We have overhead cameras that read jumps and he's off incredibly quick," Scioscia said, according to David Rice of FanSided.com. "From a scouting perspective, there is no question this guy is one of the best center fielders in our game. The ground he covers is unbelievable."

So is the ground he has forced other outfielders to cover. Their problem was that they could not catch balls hit over the fence. Trout led the American League in slugging percentage in 2017. Injuries wiped out 48 games of his season, but he still belted 33 home runs.

QUICK FACT

The Angels were among the top draws in MLB before and after the arrival of Mike Trout. They exceeded three million in attendance every year from 2003 through 2017, according to Baseball Reference.

Most experts agreed that Trout was the best player in baseball. But he had little desire to be the most marketable. His modest upbringing and humble nature ensured other priorities in his life.

CHAPTER FOUR

Outside of Baseball

Mike Trout wanted to ask high school sweetheart Jessica Cox to marry him. But he wanted to do it in a special way. So he popped the question without saying a word.

Trout receives the 2016 Silver Slugger Award at a ceremony in April 2017. He poses with his parents; his fiancée, Jessica (*third from left*); Angels manager Mike Scioscia (*left*); and members of the team's staff.

It was July 2, 2016. The couple was in Boston, Massachusetts, where the Angels were playing the Red Sox. According to *Sports Illustrated*, Trout hired a skywriter to write "Will you marry me Jess?" She said "yes." They married in December 2017.

The event was typical Trout. He has a passion for airplane emojis. His love for his longtime girlfriend is tied to his love for his hometown. And Millville has proven its love for him. The New Jersey town has gone through its struggles. Trout has remained a source of pride throughout the hardest of times.

"Mikey is what keeps our heart beating here," former Millville mayor and Trout family neighbor Tim Shannon told Bob Nightengale. "We've gone through some tough times with the unemployment, crime, and factories closing, but what keeps our excitement going is Mike."

The population of Millville is just 28,000. Nearly one-third turned out to watch Trout play for the first time in Philadelphia in 2014. He received a standing ovation before his first at-bat.

That ovation was not for Mike Trout the baseball player. It was for Mike Trout the person. It

Fans in Philadelphia awaited the arrival of Trout in hopes of getting his autograph before the Angels played the Phillies in May 2014.

Mike Trout pets a dog during a fund-raiser to benefit an animal shelter before a September 2016 game against the Toronto Blue Jays.

was for the man who gave his parents enough money to retire. It was for the man who purchased a home nearby so he could stay in Millville. It was for the man who gives his time and money to the Big Brothers Big Sisters program. It was for the man who signs autographs for kids before every game. It was for the man who visits sick children in the hospital.

> **QUICK FACT**
>
> **Meteorology is a hobby for Trout. He has made appearances on the Weather Channel. A network meteorologist even sent him a weather balloon as a gift, according to Fox Sports.**
>
> HOME 0 5 0 0 0 0 0 0 2 1

The DeSimone family of nearby Buena Vista, New Jersey, learned all about that Mike Trout. Their house burned down before Christmas in 2015. Their children had no gifts. Their holiday spirit was gone. Trout heard about the tragedy. So he showed up on Christmas Eve with presents for the kids.

"It's always good to give back and try to make people happy, especially if it's in your own hometown," Trout told MLB.com. His playing the role of Santa Claus for the DeSimone children proved again his desire to help young people.

Caring About Kids

Trout has focused on kids in his charitable work. He helped raise money for underprivileged young people in 2015 by raffling off a prize called the "Mike Trout Experience." Fans bought tickets for a chance to win a Trout autographed jersey, hat, and baseball. They would also win two tickets to an Angels game and a meet-and-greet with Trout.

Proceeds of the raffle went to programs to benefit kids in American cities. They also helped people around the world in need of clean water. Trout did not leave out his beloved Millville. Some of the money went to support the athletic department at his former high school.

Trout has not just provided funds for the schools he has attended. He has also thrilled their students through personal visits. "Mike came back to ... talk to the kids [in 2012]," teacher Janet DeClementi told

Trout signed these Nike cleats before wearing them in a game against the Toronto Blue Jays at Angel Stadium. He often donates autographed shoes to charity events.

Spencer Kent of NJ.com. "Kids were on the edge of their seats ... I'm actually part of his fan club."

Such moments mean more to Trout than earning money through endorsements. But he also understands the business side of baseball. He knows the benefits of pitching products. He has endorsed BodyArmor SuperDrink since 2012. He has sponsored such popular businesses as Subway. He became the first baseball player since Hall of Famer Ken Griffey Jr. to land a signature shoe deal with Nike.

QUICK FACT

Trout's agent is former minor league player Craig Landis. Landis's father, Jim, enjoyed a long career as a fine defensive outfielder for the Chicago White Sox and other major league teams.

Rejecting the Spotlight

But Trout does nothing to bring attention to himself. He has no visible tattoo or showy hairstyle. He offers

Mike Trout is all smiles during batting practice in July 2017 as he returns from an injury that sidelined him for seven weeks.

QUICK FACT

What is Trout's favorite order at Jim's Lunch in Millville? According to Spencer Kent, it is six hamburgers with Jim's secret sauce.

no opinions on social or political issues on his Twitter account, which has more than 2.4 million followers. He does little merchandising. Still, the Angels do their best to sell their superstar. They featured four Mike Trout bobblehead nights during the 2017 season.

Trout could earn millions more during the offseason. But he would rather spend time in his beloved Millville with family and friends than fly around the country doing commercials. Some things never change.

"There's some endorsements you have to do, but for me, I try to minimize it," he told Tyler Kepner of the *New York Times*. "During the off-season, I try to get my mind off baseball as much as I can. You don't need those endorsements and photo shoots ... Maybe down the road I'll get more into it, but right now, I'm just a baseball player. I come to the ballpark, try to get better each and every day and help the team win."

He would rather hang out at Jim's Lunch in Millville. It is his favorite hamburger joint. According to Spencer Kent, it is where he can hang out with friends who love him for what he is and not for what he has achieved. They recall when Trout was a little baby in diapers and his parents would say, "This is (our) little Mikey, he's our little angel."

Now he is the great Los Angeles Angel. But he is still the same "Mikey" to the folks of Millville. He would not have it any other way.

TIMELINE

1991: Michael Nelson Trout is born on August 7 in Vineland, New Jersey.

2009: The Los Angeles Angels select Trout with the 25th pick in the first round of the MLB Draft.

2011: Trout goes 0-for-3 in his major league debut on July 8. The Angels send Trout back to the minors on August 1. Trout is promoted again to Los Angeles on August 19. He slugs two home runs in a game against Seattle on August 30.

2012: Trout plays his first game of the season for the Angels on April 28 after illness and injury had ruined his spring training. Trout achieves his first four-hit game on June 4. Orioles slugger J. J. Hardy is robbed of a home run on a leaping Trout catch on June 27. Trout ends the year leading the American League in stolen bases and runs scored. Trout wins American League Rookie of the Year honors.

2013: Trout hits a single, double, triple, and home run to achieve the cycle on May 21. Trout finishes the season atop the American League in runs and walks.

2014: The Angels sign Trout to a six-year contract worth $144 million on March 28. Trout plays a key role in helping the Angels make the playoffs in October. He wins his first American League Most Valuable Player award on November 13.

2015: Trout becomes the youngest player in baseball history to reach 100 home runs and 100 stolen bases. He reaches 40 home runs in a season for the first time on September 22.

2016: Trout finishes another MVP season leading the league in runs, walks, and on-base percentage.

2017: A thumb injury prevents Trout from making his sixth straight All-Star Game appearance on July 11.

OTHER LIVING LEGENDS OF BASEBALL

Willie Mays (1931–) is considered by many the greatest baseball player ever. He was a brilliant center fielder for the New York and San Francisco Giants who finished his career with 660 home runs. His catch in Game 1 of the 1954 World Series remains one of the finest in the history of the sport.

Hank Aaron (1934–) hit 755 home runs to break the storied career record held by Babe Ruth. The slugging outfielder starred for the Milwaukee and Atlanta Braves before finishing his incredible career with the Milwaukee Brewers in 1976.

Sandy Koufax (1935–) is perhaps the most dominant pitcher who ever lived. The Los Angeles Dodgers left-hander managed arguably the greatest run by a pitcher in history from 1962 to 1966, when he led the National League in earned run average every year and averaged more than a strikeout per inning.

Rickey Henderson (1958–) is the greatest base stealer in baseball history. His 1,406 career thefts included a record 130 in 1982 for the Oakland Athletics. Henderson was a feared leadoff hitter for his power and amazing .401 career on-base percentage.

Cal Ripken Jr. (1960–) broke the all-time record for consecutive games played with 2,632 over a 17-year period. He finished his brilliant career with 3,184 hits and two American League Most Valuable Player awards for the Baltimore Orioles.

Greg Maddux (1966–) boasted pinpoint control in pitching the Atlanta Braves to the 1995 World Series title and landing a spot in the Hall of Fame. He led the National League in earned run average four times from 1993 to 1998.

Ken Griffey Jr. (1969–) was an amazing all-around center fielder who starred with the Seattle Mariners and Cincinnati Reds. He slammed 630 career home runs despite numerous injuries that kept him off the field. His fearless defensive style resulted in many crashes against outfield walls.

Albert Pujols (1980–) slammed 2,968 hits from 2001 to 2017. Included were 614 home runs. He won the National League Rookie of the Year award in 2001 and National League Most Valuable Player honors with the St. Louis Cardinals in 2005, 2008, and 2009. He led the league in runs scored five times.

Miguel Cabrera (1983–) is considered the best pure hitter of his generation. He starred with the Florida Marlins and Detroit Tigers and won American League Most Valuable Player honors in 2012 and 2013. Cabrera won the batting title four times, in 2011, 2012, 2013, and 2015.

Clayton Kershaw (1988–) had established himself as one of the greatest left-handed pitchers in baseball history by age 26. The Los Angeles Dodgers' superstar led the National League in earned run average every season from 2011 to 2014 and again in 2017. Kershaw won the National League Cy Young Award in 2011, 2013, and 2014 and Major League Player of the Year honors in 2014.

GLOSSARY

batting average A number that shows how often a batter gets a base hit.

charitable Done or designed to help people who are poor, sick, and so forth.

debut A first-time performance at a particular level.

discipline The ability to keep working at something that is difficult.

emoji A small image, symbol, or icon used in electronic communication such as text messages, emails, and social media.

endorsement The act of publicly saying that you like or use a product or service in exchange for money.

Major League Baseball (MLB) An organization that governs professional baseball in North America. It is made up of two leagues—the American League and the National League. There are fifteen teams and three divisions in each league.

marketable Able to be sold; wanted by buyers or employers.

merchandising The activity of trying to sell goods or services through advertising or displaying them attractively.

metric A type of advanced statistic in sports used to analyze player performance.

minor leagues A collection of professional baseball teams in the United States that compete at levels below the Major League Baseball level. Minor league teams are affiliated with major league teams and used as a training ground for major league players.

no-hitter A performance in which a pitcher or pitchers allow no base hits in a baseball game.

on-base percentage The percentage of times that a batter reaches base by hit or walk.

phenom A person who is very good at doing something, such as a sport.

promotion The act of moving someone to a higher or more important position or rank in an organization.

prospect An athlete with strong potential.
rookie A first-year player in a professional sport.
runs batted in (RBI) A statistic that counts the number of runs that score as a result of a player's at-bats.
skeptical Having or expressing doubt about something.
slugging percentage The number of total bases of a hitter divided by his number of at-bats.
tendinitis A painful condition in which a tendon in an arm, leg, or other part of the body becomes inflamed.
underprivileged Having fewer advantages, privileges, and opportunities than most people.

FOR MORE INFORMATION

Books

Bechtel, Mark. *Big Book of WHO: Baseball*. New York, NY: Liberty Street, 2017.

Christopher, Matt. *Play Ball!* (Little League). New York, NY: Little, Brown Books for Young Readers, 2013.

Dzidrums, Christine. *Mike Trout: Baseball Sensation* (Sportstars). Whittier, CA: Creative Media, 2013.

Fishman, Jon M. *Mike Trout* (Amazing Athletes). Minneapolis, MN: Lerner Publications, 2014.

Gilbert, Sara. *The Story of the Los Angeles Angels of Anaheim*. Mankato, MN: Creative Education, 2011.

Gitlin, Marty. *Baseball Legends in the Making*. North Mankato, MN: Capstone Press, 2014.

Green, Tim. *Force Out*. New York, NY: Harper, 2014.

Green, Tim. *New Kid*. New York, NY: Harper, 2015.

Gutman, Dan. *Willie & Me* (A Baseball Card Adventure). New York, NY: Harper, 2016.

Jacobs, Greg. *The Everything Kids' Baseball Book: From Baseball's History to Today's Favorite Players—With Lots of Home Run Fun in Between!* Avon, MA: Adams Media, 2016.

Jeter, Derek. *Fair Ball*. New York, NY: Simon & Schuster Books for Young Readers, 2017.

Kelley, K. C. *Baseball Superstars 2016*. New York, NY: Scholastic Inc., 2016.

Morreale, Marie. *Mike Trout* (Real Bios). New York, NY: Children's Press, 2016.

Rice, Dona. *Batter Up! History of Baseball*. Huntington Beach, CA: Teacher Created Materials, 2014.

Shang, Wendy Wan-Long. *The Way Home Looks Now*. New York, NY: Scholastic Inc., 2017.

Websites

Baseball Reference
https://www.baseball-reference.com/players/t/troutmi01.shtml

Major League Baseball Official Site of the Los Angeles Angels of Anaheim
http://m.mlb.com/player/545361/mike-trout

Sports Illustrated
https://www.si.com/node/483646

INDEX

M

N

O

P

R

S

T

V

W